A GIFT BOOK
For Girl Dads

To: _____

A Celebration of YOU!

♥

And All You Mean to Me

Love: _____

I Am a GIRL!

What's Your Super Power?

I Am
a GIRL,

With a

GIRL

DAD!

A PICTURE OF MY DAD AND ME

LUCKY ME, DAD! I GOT YOU!!!

All the ways you help empower me to be my best self:

_____

_____

_____

_____

_____

_____

_____

_____

_____

_____

_____

BEST DADDY SONG

The idea for "Best Daddy" came to me a couple of years after my daughter was born. I noodled with the tune over many years until one day, I was singing the chorus in the kitchen and she playfully sang it back to me.

There was a "call and response" game that transpired between us and she sang a slightly different version of the melody back to me that ended up being a harmony that helped complete the song.

Now when we play the song, she smiles at me knowing she helped catalyze it coming into the world. It's special for her and for us. I see her light up with confidence about all she has to offer the world.

This song reminds me of what is most important to me. As the songs says, "I might never drive a Caddy, but I'm gonna be the BEST DADDY I can be.

~ Cody Qualls

Award Winning - Internationally recognized singer/songwriter

Stream search "Best Daddy Cody Qualls" or Purchase song at CodyQualls.com

"Best Daddy"

This is the kinda song you don't hear every day
So many things I used to want have faded away
I used to only think about myself in a way
But you be revealing a deeper purpose in me

And people say I've changed, I tell them gladly
Puttin' my attention on my family
I might never drizzy drive that caddy
but I'm gonna be the best daddy, I can be

You are the best daddy!
You are the best daddy! (kids sing)
My kids tell me, you are the best daddy!

When I'm walkin in the door comin' home for the day
When I'm tired I need renewal from my family
You be pleading, Daddy please don't push it too hard
You remindin' this man, that he's worthy of love

chorus

Dad we're sad when you have to go
But we'll be here when you get home
Bring me something back you know
Cause I'll be here when you get home

Made By Sophie

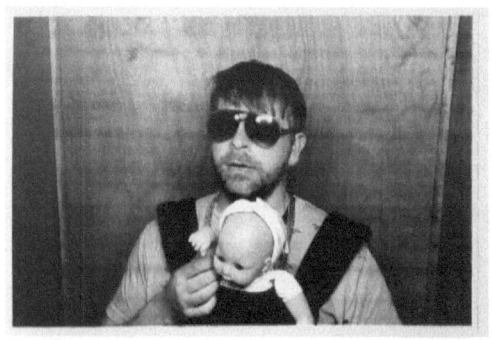

Dear Dad,

I love you because...

You have a loving heart
You check your pecks in the mirror all the time
You sometimes resemble a gorilla
But always look like Zach Galafinakis

You are passionate, often obsessive and love adventure
You are a great dad and person
You tend to have bald friends
You cry at stuff as simple as house hunters

You are definitely the smarter parent
Your love for learning is inspirational
Your bald spot is growing and I am worried
We have had a lot of fun times together

I love you Dad

Sophie
United States

Dear Tato:

Thank you for adopting me and giving me a wonderful life that I would have never known if I had stayed in that orphanage. You rescued me from the despair of wanting to be wanted.

When you walked in the door that day and you took my new born baby sister into your arms to take her home, I ran up and threw my arms around your leg. You took one look at me and swept me up into your other arm and hugged me tight.

That day you chose me too.

I am forever grateful.

You are our Girl Dad Angel!

        Love,

        Tatiana
        Ukraine/Australia

My Father Always Said to Me,

"I am the bow and you are the arrow.

It is my honor and purpose to help you soar as far and as high as you dream of going."

Winona
The Oldest Daughter
First Nations
Canada

WHAT I LOVE MOST ABOUT WHO YOU ARE, DAD

Women for Women International
Replica of a card made from banana leaves from Rwanda

Dear Baba:

I am so grateful that you are sending me to this girl's school so I can have a better life in the future. Because of you and the sacrifices you have made, I won't have to be married before I'm 13 and have children when I'm still a child myself.

I know you miss me when I'm gone
and
I miss you too.

The gift of having an education was my only dream and it makes me very happy to be here learning. I can have a very different life than other girls in my village because of the sacrifices you're making.

I promise to take advantage of every opportunity to share my gifts with the world after I receive my diploma.

Ashe,

Naipanoi
Africa

Paulus Rusyanto/Dreamstime.com

Dear Dad:

You are no longer with me here on earth, but I always remember you reading me this quote from my Winnie the Pooh books when I was a little girl.

It has comforted me and raised me up through the years since you passed on to be in the LIGHT.

"If ever there is a tomorrow, when we're not together.

There is something you must always remember.

You are BRAVER than you believe,
STRONGER than you seem,
And SMARTER than you think.

But the most important thing is, even if we're apart,
I'll ALWAYS be with you."

~ A.A. Milne

I am so thankful for your unconditional love and belief in me. I am a lucky woman to have had such a present, loving and encouraging Girl Dad.

I walk in the world with dignity, self-respect, confidence and strength that a lot of women don't have. You left a legacy of what every father should be and I feel your presence, support and guidance often even now Dad. I miss you so much.

Your little girl forever,

Elizabeth
United Kingdom

You're In Good Company, Dad

<u>Celebrity Girl Dads</u>

Adam Sandler
Alex Rodriguez
Barack Obama
Bono
Breckin Meyer
Bruce Willis
Chris Brown
Chris Rock
Clint Eastwood
Dave Bautista
Dave Grohl
David Beckham
Dax Shephard
Dierks Bentley
Dwayne "The Rock" Johnson
Dwyane Wade
Eric Dane
George Stephanopoulos
George W. Bush
Harry Connick Jr
Jamie Dornan
Jamie Foxx
John Krasinski
John Legend
Judd Apatow
Kanye West
Keith Urban

Kyle Rudolph
Lenny Kravitz
Lionel Richie
Mario Lopez
Matt Damon
Michael Strahan
Mick Fleetwood
Paul McCartney
Peter Facinelli
Peter Sarsgaard
Phil Collins
Ron Howard
Russell Simmons
Russell Wilson
Ryan Gosling
Ryan Reynolds
Sidney Poitier
Sylvester Stallone
Steph Curry
Sterling Shepard
Tim McGraw
Timbaland
Travis Scott
William H Macy

<u>And in Memoriam of Kobe Bryant</u>
Girl Dad to four daughters, who died being a dad to Gigi doing what his daughter loved most.

A Legacy of Love and Support!

A Father Is His Daughter's
First Love

I feel safe snuggled against your imposing stature, or embraced by your endless arms. My heart tenses when I realize that soon, too soon, I would be huddled against someone else who is still unknown to me, that I would be embraced by someone other than you. Someone with whom I hope I will feel just as safe and just as good as I feel with you Dad. I will never replace you. Never! I love so much about you. The way your eyes close when you laugh. The way you never give up while playing tennis or when you're trying to teach me something. The way you always listen to me without interrupting and are always here for me. Thanks to you, I know I'm ready to face all I will encounter during the course that leads me to my future. Ready to fight and defend myself, ready to win and succeed. I am so so so proud of being your daughter and the reason I feel so prepared is because of the impact you have had on me.
Thank you! I love you.

                        Yours Forever,
                        ~ Penny
                          Singapore

My Dad makes me feel special by always believing and supporting me in the moments when I need it the most. When I thought I was failing in a sport, he helped me gain strength and courage, and by making me resilient has taught me that in life there will be hard things that don't always turn out the way I want them to, and I cannot give up on the things that matter to me.

I cannot thank you enough Dad for always being there for me, reassuring me and trusting me. Thank you for brightening my days with your cute smile that always makes me feel warm inside. I love you to the moon and back. Thanks for bringing me to life.

              Lots of love to the best Dad ever!
                    xx Estelle xx
                      Milan

I grow strong
in the shade of your tree

and

stand tall
because of the roots you
nourish.

MEMORIES I'LL NEVER FORGET, DAD

_____

_____

_____

_____

_____

_____

_____

_____

_____

_____

_____

_____

_____

_____

_____

_____

_____

_____ ♥

Thank you for all the magical times together!

You Can't Scare Me!

I HAVE TWO DAUGHTERS,

a WIFE,

a GIRL DOG,

and a MARE!

~Lars, Swedish Girl Dad

Dear Dad,

Thank you for always believing in me even when I don't believe in myself. You have pushed me to be the best that I can be in everything I do. You have been to all my soccer and basketball games cheering for me on the sidelines. You talk to me during halftime and help me understand what I can do better. Even when I get hard on myself or on you, you're still by my side.

I know you're always proud of me whether I win or lose. I am so happy that we have such a good relationship, you are my best friend. When my team loses an important game in basketball, you are there telling us that we did amazing and how we should be so proud of ourselves. Thanks, Dad!

I love you,

Audrey #1

WE CELEBRATE ALL GIRL DADS!

Their daughters have greater self-esteem and self-respect which impacts the partners they choose, the dreams they pursue and their beliefs about what they deserve.

GIRL DADS ARE CHANGING THE WORLD!

As these women will thrive in their life and work!

GIRL
DADS

GirlDadsBook.com

Visit our site to participate in a Research Survey for our next book Girl Dads: Changing the World.

Highlighting the social shifts around fatherhood, parenting and masculinity. Girl dads embrace a new model where men are blending their heads and hearts, and where loving kindness, and empathy are signs of strength.

www.ingramcontent.com/pod-product-compliance
Lightning Source LLC
Chambersburg PA
CBHW020432010526
44118CB00010B/542